"Il vero lusso di una mensa sta nel dessert"
The real luxury of a meal lies in the dessert.
From *Il Piacere* by Gabriele D'Annunzio

ANNA DEL CONTE'S

Italian Kitchen

I DOLCI

SWEET THINGS

ILLUSTRATED BY FLO BAYLEY

SIMON &
SCHUSTER

**SIMON &
SCHUSTER**

SIMON & SCHUSTER
Simon & Schuster Building
Rockefeller Center
1230 Avenue of the Americas
New York, New York 10020

Designed by Andrew Barron & Collis Clements Associates
Typesetting by Selwood Systems, Midsomer Norton, Avon
Printed and bound in Italy by New Interlitho

10 9 8 7 6 5 4 3 2 1

Library of Congress Cataloging in Publication Data
Del Conte, Anna.
   I dolci : sweet things / by Anna del Conte.
      p.   cm. — (Anna del Conte's Italian kitchen)
   Includes bibliographical references and index.
   ISBN 0–671–87032–7 : $14.00
   1. Desserts—Italy.   2. Cookery, Italian.   I. Title.
   II. Series: Del Conte, Anna.   Anna del Conte's Italian
kitchen.
   TX773.D344   1993
   641.8'6—dc20
                                            93–17493
                                            CIP

CONTENTS

DOLCI

Italians love desserts, although they only eat them on special occasions. An everyday meal ends with fresh fruit; desserts are kept for Sundays, parties, family gatherings, religious days, and village *feste*.

Dolci developed differently in northern, central, and southern Italy. The dolci of the North are often little more than sweet breads, the panettone milanese being the prime sample. The dolci of central Italy are richer, with lots of spices, nuts, candied peel, and honey, as in the panforte from Siena or the *certosino* from Bologna. It was also in this part of the country that there originated the "*dolci al cucchiaio*" (desserts that can be eaten with a spoon such as the *zuppe inglesi*, or trifles) of Emilia-Romagna and Tuscany. In southern Italy, the protagonists of dolci are almonds and candied fruits, a heritage from Arab cooking. And it is here that dolci reach the highest level of culinary art.

This being Italy, there are, of course, many exceptions to this rule. After all, the birthplace of zabaglione – the *dolce al cucchiaio* par excellence – is Piedmont in the North, while a *ciambella* – sweet ring-shaped bread made with potatoes, eggs, and flour – is a traditional dolce of Apulia.

As they are eaten on feast days, dolci are even more regional than other kinds of food. Every patron saint, every feast day of the year, has its own special dolce, in every town in Italy. The region that has more special occasions and more legends associated with its dolci is Sicily. There are cookies called *frutti di morte* – fruits of death – made with *pasta reale* – almond paste – that are eaten at the end of a meal on All Soul's day, November 2. The *sfinci di San Giuseppe* are a sort of fritter eaten on St Joseph's day, March 19. For Easter Sunday, a magnificent *agnello pasquale* – Easter lamb – is made in Sicily with a pastry, strongly flavored with cloves, that is molded in the shape of a lamb.

Some of these special dolci have become so popular that they are now eaten all year round, not only in Italy but abroad, as is the case with panettone and panforte, both originally eaten only at Christmas. When I was in Sicily recently, I ate some superb soft cookies called *olivette di Sant'Agata*. They were made of marzipan, sugar, rum, and vanilla, and are a specialty of Catania, made originally on the saint's day of Sant'Agata, a local martyr. I had never heard of *olivette* before, yet they are the best almond-based cookies I have ever had. Our Sicilian hostess insisted that we drive many, many miles along the free-way to an old-fashioned *pasticceria* in Catania to buy "the only *olivette* worth eating." The lengths the Italians will go in their search for excellence, as far as food is concerned, never ceases to amaze me.

The tradition of excellence in Italian dolci goes back a long way. Writing in Naples at the beginning of the nineteenth century, Lady Blessington, a friend of Emma Hamilton, commented "Italian confectionery and ices are far superior to those of the French and the English, and their variety is infinite." A passage from *Il Gattopardo* by Giuseppe Tomasi di Lampedusa gives a good idea of what Lady Blessington meant. He describes how, at the great ball, the table was covered with "pink parfaits, champagne parfaits, gray parfaits which parted creaking under the blade of the cake knife; a violin melody in major of candied morello cherries; acid notes of yellow pineapples; and the *trionfi della gola* – triumphs of gluttony – with the opaque green of their pistachio paste, and the shameless *minni di virgini* – virgins' breasts."

TORTE E CROSTATE

CAKES AND TARTS

The emphasis of this section is on cakes containing fruit and nuts.

In Italy, cakes, even the drier sort, are often eaten as part of a meal. Cakes are also served mid-morning or after supper, when they are traditionally accompanied by a glass of wine. Wine, after all, used to be the cheapest beverage, one that even poor people in the country could afford. They made their own wine, while tea or coffee had to be bought.

The section ends with two recipes for tarts. Tarts are not as common in Italy as in France, but the ones I have chosen are very characteristic and, so far as I know, are only to be found in their place of origin.

In all the cake and cookie recipes, I recommend the use of Italian 00 flour. This is a high-quality flour with very little flavor and very good raising properties. It is available from specialist Italian stores.

TORTA DI PERE E BANANE

PEAR AND BANANA PIE

Serves 8

1 unwaxed lemon
2 large, ripe but firm, good
quality pears, about 1 pound
2 large bananas
unsalted butter for the pan
2 tablespoons all-purpose flour
1½ tablespoons sugar

For the pastry

1⅔ cups all-purpose flour,
preferably Italian 00 (see
page 7)
1 teaspoon baking powder
½ teaspoon salt
½ cup sugar
1 stick unsalted butter, cut into
small pieces
1 egg yolk
2–4 tablespoons milk

Some Italian pies and tarts are made with a pastry that is quite soft, halfway between a short pastry and a sponge cake. This is because baking powder is added to the pastry dough. It is particularly suitable for pies, when it envelops a moist filling, as in this recipe.

1 Scrub and dry the lemon, then grate the zest. Squeeze the juice.
2 To make the pastry dough, sift the flour with the baking powder and salt onto a work surface. Mix in half the grated lemon zest and the sugar, then rub in the butter. Add the egg yolk and enough milk to bind to a dough. (You can make the pastry dough in a food processor, but be careful when you add the milk.) Form a ball, wrap, and chill at least 2 hours.
3 Peel the pears. Cut into quarters, remove cores, and then cut into chunks. Put in a bowl and add the lemon juice and the remaining zest.
4 Peel the bananas and cut into slices. Add to the pears and mix well. Let macerate about 30 minutes.
5 Heat the oven to 350°F.
6 Lightly butter a 9-inch loose-based tart pan.
7 Mix the flour with the sugar.
8 Cut off about two-thirds of the dough and roll it out into a circle large enough to cover the bottom and sides of the pan. Press gently into the pan. Sprinkle two-thirds of the flour and sugar mixture over the dough. With a slotted spoon, transfer the fruit to the pastry shell, leaving juices behind in the bowl. Sprinkle the remaining flour and sugar mixture over the fruit.
9 Roll out the rest of the dough to cover the pie and place over the fruit. Seal the edge, pressing down with the prongs of a fork.

Make a few holes on the surface with the fork for the steam to escape.

10 Place the pan in the oven. Bake until golden. 50–60 minutes.

11 Let the pie cool in the pan and then carefully unmold and transfer to a serving plate.

If you are serving the pie at the end of a meal, a bowl of whipped cream goes well with it.

TORTA DI MELE
APPLE CAKE

When I was in Italy recently, I asked my cousin Mariella for a recipe for an apple cake. All my cousins are good cooks, and some of my recipes come from them. Back home, a few months later, I found no less than five recipes for Mariella's apple cakes. Very disturbing. But only one was marked *"Buonissima,"* so I began with this one and have never bothered with the others.

It certainly is very good, with its homey appearance yet rich buttery base, which is covered with a thick layer of very thin slices of lemon-flavored apples. This type of cake is not served with cream in Italy, not for health reasons, but because it is better without.

---

1 Peel the apples. Cut into quarters, remove the core, and slice thinly. Put the slices in a bowl. Add the lemon juice and mix the apple slices so that they all share the juice. Let macerate while you prepare the cake batter.

2 Beat the egg yolks with the granulated sugar until pale and mousse-like. Add the butter and stir until totally incorporated.

Serves 8

2 pounds apples
juice of 1 lemon
2 extra large eggs, separated
$\frac{3}{4}$ cup granulated sugar
1 stick unsalted butter, melted
1 cup all-purpose flour,
preferably Italian 00 (see
page 7)
1 tablespoon baking powder
$\frac{1}{2}$ teaspoon salt
unsalted butter and dry bread
crumbs for the pan

To finish
2 tablespoons unsalted butter,
melted
confectioners' sugar

3 Heat the oven to 350°F.

4 Sift together the flour, baking powder, and salt.

5 Beat the egg whites until stiff but not dry. Sprinkle 2 tablespoons of the flour mixture over the egg mixture and fold it in with 2 tablespoons of the beaten egg whites. Repeat this addition of flour and egg white, folding them in very gently with a high movement.

6 Butter a 10-inch spring form cake pan and sprinkle with bread crumbs to coat the bottom and sides. Throw away excess crumbs. Spoon the cake batter into the pan and cover with layers of sliced apple.

7 Pour the melted butter all over the apple slices and place the pan in the oven. This cake takes at least 1 hour to bake. If it is browning too much at the edge, turn the heat down a little and continue baking until the middle is cooked. Test by inserting a wooden toothpick; it should come out dry.

8 Turn the pan over on to a wire rack, remove the clip band and the base of the pan, and let the cake cool. When cold, turn the cake over onto a round serving-plate and sprinkle lavishly with sifted confectioners sugar. Do this just before serving or the sugar will soak into the cake and disappear.

TORTA DI CIOCCOLATO FARCITA DI ZABAIONE

—— CHOCOLATE AND ZABAGLIONE CAKE ——

Serves 8

2 ounces semisweet chocolate
7 tablespoons unsalted butter,
at room temperature
$\frac{3}{4}$ cup & 2 tablespoons sugar
3 extra large eggs, at room
temperature, separated
$1\frac{1}{2}$ tablespoons dark rum
$\frac{2}{3}$ cup all-purpose flour, preferably
Italian 00 (see page 7)
$\frac{3}{4}$ cup potato flour
$1\frac{1}{2}$ teaspoons baking powder
$1\frac{1}{2}$ teaspoons salt
1 teaspoon lemon juice
unsalted butter and flour for
the pan
$\frac{2}{3}$ cup whipping cream

For the zabaglione
4 extra large egg yolks
$\frac{1}{3}$ cup sugar
a piece of vanilla bean
$\frac{1}{2}$ cup dry Marsala or
medium sherry wine

My editor, Gillian Young, sampled this cake when she came to tea the other day, and declared it very well worth writing about. This endorsed my opinion, because it has the perfect balance of chocolate, sugar, and alcohol. The zabaglione, poured on each half of the cake, partly sinks into the sponge. This makes a thin layer in the middle of the cake, giving it two slightly different textures.

Like many Italian cooks, I often replace half the all-purpose flour with the same amount of potato flour for more lightness in the cake; it is these quantities which are given below.

1 Heat the oven to 250°F. Break the chocolate into small pieces, put in a heatproof bowl, and warm in the oven until the chocolate has melted. Set the chocolate aside. Turn the oven heat up to 375°F.

2 Beat the butter until it is soft. Add the sugar and beat together until pale and creamy. Gradually beat in the egg yolks, rum, and melted chocolate.

3 Sift the two flours, baking powder, and salt together twice.

4 Beat the egg whites with the lemon juice until stiff but not dry. (The lemon juice, being acid, helps to stabilize the froth without increasing its volume.)

5 Add 1 tablespoon of the flour mixture and 1 tablespoon of the egg white and fold into the chocolate mixture with a high movement, using a metal spoon. Continue adding alternate spoonfuls of flour mixture and egg white.

6 Generously butter an 8-inch springform cake pan. Sprinkle with flour, then shake out excess. Spoon the cake batter into the pan and place in the oven. The cake will be cooked in about 45 minutes. To see if it is ready, insert a wooden toothpick into the middle; it should come out dry.

7 Let the cake settle in the pan about 10 minutes, then unmold it onto a wire rack to cool.

8 Meanwhile, make the zabaglione. Put the egg yolks, sugar, and vanilla in a round-bottomed metal bowl or in the upper part of a double boiler. Beat well with a small balloon whisk. Beat in the Marsala. Set the bowl in a bain-marie, i.e. in a pan containing simmering water, or set the double boiler pan over the bottom pan. Continue beating until the mixture is dense and thick.

9 Cut the cake horizontally in half. Make some slits in the cut face of each layer and pour about two-thirds of the zabaglione all over them. Do this slowly to allow the zabaglione to penetrate into the cake. Put the two layers together again. Refrigerate for at least 6 hours.

10 Whip the cream until stiff. Whisk the rest of the zabaglione until it is thick again, then mix evenly with the cream. Cover the top of the cake with this mixture. Keep the cake in the refrigerater until you want to serve it.

TORTA DI CIOCCOLATO CON LE PERE
CHOCOLATE AND PEAR CAKE

Serves 4–6

2½ ounces semisweet chocolate, broken into small pieces
5 tablespoons unsalted butter, at room temperature
½ cup & 2 tablespoons confectioners' sugar, sifted
1 egg, at room temperature, separated
2 egg yolks, at room temperature
pinch of ground cinnamon
pinch of salt
1 large, ripe but firm, Bartlett pear, about ½ pound
¾ cup all-purpose flour, preferably Italian 00 (see page 7)
unsalted butter and flour for the pan
confectioners' sugar, for decoration

I make this cake in a loaf pan, as it used to be made at home for our *merenda* – afternoon tea. If you want to serve it as a dessert, I suggest making it in a 6-inch round pan.

1 Heat the oven to 250°F. Put the chocolate in a heatproof bowl and melt it in the oven. Remove from the oven and keep in a warm place. Turn the oven heat up to 350°F.

2 Beat the butter until really soft. I use a hand-held electric mixer. Gradually add the confectioners' sugar while beating constantly, then beat until light and pale yellow. (If you add all the sugar at once and start beating butter and sugar together, you will find the sugar flying everywhere except in the butter.) Add the 3 egg yolks, cinnamon, salt, and melted chocolate.

3 Beat the egg white until stiff but not dry and then fold it into the butter mixture by the spoonful, alternating it with spoonfuls of flour. Fold lightly but thoroughly.

4 Peel and core the pear and cut it into ½-inch cubes. Mix lightly into the batter.

5 Butter a loaf pan that is approximately 7 × 4 × 2 inches. Sprinkle in 1 tablespoon of flour, shake the pan so the flour covers all the surface, and then throw away the excess flour. Spoon the cake batter into the pan. Bake until the sides of the cake have shrunk from the pan, about 50 minutes. The cake should be dry in the middle – test by inserting a wooden toothpick.

6 Remove the pan from the oven, unmold the cake onto a wire rack, and let it cool.

7 Sprinkle with sifted confectioners' sugar just before serving.

Torta di Noci
Walnut Cake

Serves 6–8

1 stick unsalted butter, at room temperature
1¼ cups confectioners' sugar, sifted
3 extra large eggs, at room temperature, separated
1 cup walnut pieces
¾ cup all-purpose flour, preferably Italian 00 (see page 7)
½ tablespoon baking powder
pinch of salt
grated zest of 1 lemon
¼ teaspoon lemon juice
unsalted butter and dry bread crumbs for the pan
confectioners' sugar, for decoration

Buy your walnuts from a shop with a quick turnover so that they will not be old and rancid. Better still, buy the nuts in their shells at Christmas time and shell them yourself. Keep them in the freezer.

1 Heat the oven to 350°F.

2 Beat the butter until very soft. Gradually beat in confectioners' sugar to make a smooth, thick cream. Use a hand-held electric mixer, if you have one.

3 Lightly beat the egg yolks together with a fork, then add gradually to the butter cream, mixing thoroughly to incorporate.

4 Put the walnuts in a food processor and process until very coarsely ground while pulsing the machine. If you do not have a processor, chop by hand. The nuts should be grainy, not ground fine. Stir into the butter mixture.

5 Sift the flour, baking powder, and salt together and fold into the butter mixture with the lemon zest.

6 Beat the egg whites with the lemon juice until stiff but not dry and fold into the mixture, using a metal spoon and lifting it high to incorporate more air.

7 Generously butter an 8-inch spring form cake pan. Sprinkle with bread crumbs, shake the pan to cover all the surface, and then shake out excess crumbs. Spoon the cake batter into the prepared pan.

8 Bake in the preheated oven until the cake is done, about 45 minutes. Test by inserting a wooden toothpick into the middle of the cake; it should come out dry. Unclip the side band and turn the cake over onto a wire rack to cool.

9 Sprinkle lavishly with sifted confectioners' sugar before serving.

TORTA DI RICOTTA
RICOTTA CAKE

I do believe that some of the best recipes come from family *ricettari* – recipe collections. These are recipes for dishes that are suited to home cooking, and have been tested and improved over the years by generations of cooks. This is such a recipe.

1 Soak the golden raisins in hot water for 15 minutes to puff them up.

2 Reserve 1 tablespoon of the granulated sugar. Beat the butter with the remaining granulated sugar until pale and creamy and then add the eggs, one at a time. When all the eggs have been incorporated, mix in the lemon zest, potato flour, baking powder, and salt.

3 Heat the oven to 350°F.

4 Press the ricotta through the small-hole disk of a food mill, or through a strainer, directly onto the other ingredients. Do not use a food processor as this would not aereate the ricotta. Fold the ricotta thoroughly into the mixture. Drain the raisins, pat them dry with paper towels, and fold into the mixture.

5 Generously butter a 10-inch springform cake pan and sprinkle with the reserved granulated sugar to coat the bottom and sides.

6 Spoon the ricotta batter into the pan and bake until the cake is done (it will shrink slightly from the sides of the tin, $1-1\frac{1}{4}$ hours.) Let it cool in the pan. Unmold the cake when cold and place on a serving plate. Sprinkle with plenty of sifted confectioners' sugar just before serving.

Serves 10–12

$\frac{2}{3}$ cup golden raisins
$1\frac{1}{2}$ cups granulated sugar
1 stick unsalted butter, at room temperature
4 extra large eggs, at room temperature
grated zest of 1 unwaxed lemon
6 tablespoons potato flour
1 tablespoon baking powder
$\frac{1}{2}$ teaspoon salt
$2\frac{1}{4}$ pounds fresh ricotta cheese ($4\frac{1}{2}$ cups)
unsalted butter for the pan
confectioners' sugar, for decoration

LA TORTA SBRISOLONA
CRUMBLY CAKE

Serves 6

¾ cup almonds
½ cup & 2 tablespoons
granulated sugar
1 cup all-purpose flour
1 cup coarse yellow cornmeal
grated zest of 1 unwaxed lemon
pinch of salt
2 egg yolks
1 stick unsalted butter, at room
temperature
unsalted butter for the pan
confectioners' sugar, for
decoration

The word *sbrisolona* is derived from *briciola* (stress on the first syllable), meaning "crumb", which is what this cake seems to consist of. If you want it less crumbly, you can cut it into slices with a sharp knife when it is still hot. But I find that part of its appeal is its rustic appearance, as well, of course, as its deliciousness. My husband's comment on it, as he munched, was, "This cake is not just delicious – once you start eating it, you can't stop."

It is an ideal cake to take with tea or coffee in the afternoon, or with sweet wine at any time of day.

1 Heat the oven to 400°F.

2 Drop the almonds into a pan of boiling water and boil for 30 seconds after the water has come back to a boil. Drain and remove the skin by squeezing the almonds between your fingers. Spread them on a baking sheet and toast them in the oven until golden brown, about 7 minutes. Turn the heat down to 350°F.

3 Put the almonds in a food processor with 2 tablespoons of the granulated sugar and process until they are reduced to a coarse powder.

4 In a bowl, mix the flour, cornmeal, the remaining granulated sugar, lemon zest, ground almonds, and salt. Add the egg yolks and work your hands until the mixture is crumbly.

5 Add the butter to the crumbly mixture and work again to incorporate it thoroughly, until the dough sticks together in crumbly mass.

6 Generously butter an 8-inch round layer cake pan and line the bottom with parchment paper. Spread the batter evenly in the pan, pressing it down with your hands. Bake until the cake is golden brown and a skewer inserted in the center comes out dry, 40–45 minutes.

7 Unmold the cake onto a wire rack and peel off the parchment paper. Let it cool. Before serving, sprinkle the cake with sifted confectioners' sugar.

This cake will keep very well several days.

PANFORTE

SPICY CAKE FROM SIENA

Serves 8–10

2 ounces candied fruit
2 ounces preserved ginger
5 ounces mixed candied orange, lemon, and citron peel
$\frac{2}{3}$ cup ground hazelnuts
$\frac{3}{4}$ cup whole hazelnuts
$\frac{2}{3}$ cup almonds
$\frac{1}{2}$ cup walnut pieces
1 teaspoon ground cinnamon
$\frac{1}{8}$ teaspoon freshly grated nutmeg
$\frac{1}{8}$ teaspoon ground cloves
$\frac{1}{8}$ teaspoon freshly ground white pepper
$\frac{1}{8}$ teaspoon ground ginger
$\frac{1}{8}$ teaspoon ground coriander
$\frac{1}{4}$ cup all-purpose flour
1 tablespoon unsweetened cocoa powder
$\frac{1}{4}$ cup granulated sugar
$\frac{1}{4}$ cup clear honey
oil and rice paper for the pan
1 tablespoon confectioners' sugar

Panforte is one of the most ancient dolci. A reference to "a spicy and honeyed bread" brought back to Siena from the Middle East appears in Dante's *Inferno*. It is the traditional Christmas cake of Siena, but is now available all the year round.

There are two kinds of panforte, a white panforte and a black one. The white is the older version. The black was created when cocoa arrived from the New World and became the fashionable ingredient.

My recipe contains a little cocoa and makes a softer panforte than the commercial one. I have also substituted preserved ginger for candied pumpkin, which is not widely available outside Italy. The ginger is an excellent substitute, both for its flavor and by being in keeping with the early origins of panforte, when spices, just arrived from the Orient, were used very prodigally as a show of wealth.

1 Heat the oven to 350°F.

2 Coarsely chop all the candied fruit and peel and place in a bowl. (This can be done in a food processor: cut the candied fruits and peel into pieces, put in the food processor, and process for a short time, while shaking the machine backward and forward. Do not reduce to a paste.)

3 Spread the ground hazelnuts and the whole hazelnuts on two baking sheets. Toast the ground hazelnuts in the oven about 5 minutes and the whole hazelnuts 10 minutes. Shake the sheets gently from time to time. Add the ground hazelnuts to the candied fruits in the bowl.

4 Let the whole hazelnuts cool slightly and then rub them, a few at a time, in a coarse towel to remove the skin. Place the nuts in a strainer and shake to separate the skin from the nuts. Chop the nuts coarsely and add to the bowl.

5 Chop the almonds and walnuts coarsely and add to the bowl.

6 Put aside $\frac{1}{2}$ teaspoon of the cinnamon. Sift the rest of the cinnamon, all the other spices, the flour, and cocoa powder directly into the bowl. Mix well.

7 Put the granulated sugar and honey into a small saucepan. Cook over low heat until the sugar has completely dissolved. Add to the bowl and mix very well with your hands.

8 Line the bottom of a 7-inch loose-based tart pan with rice paper and grease the sides of the pan with oil. Press the mixture evenly into the pan, let stand at room temperature for 5 hours, or longer if possible.

9 Preheat the oven to 325°F.

10 Put the remaining cinnamon and the confectioners' sugar in a strainer or sifter and sprinkle over the top of the cake. Bake about 50 minutes.

11 Remove from the oven and let cool 10 minutes, then remove the panforte from the pan and cool completely on a wire rack. When cold, wrap in foil and store.

Panforte will keep at least 2–3 months.

PASTIERA NAPOLETANA

NEAPOLITAN TART

Serves 8–10

9 ounces dried whole wheat, to
be soaked, or 14 ounces
canned cooked wheat
$2\frac{1}{2}$ cups whole milk
pinch of salt
grated zest of $\frac{1}{2}$ lemon and
$\frac{1}{2}$ orange
$\frac{1}{2}$ teaspoon ground cinnamon
piece of vanilla bean, about 2-
inches long, or a few drops of
pure vanilla extract
10 ounces fresh ricotta cheese
($1\frac{1}{4}$ cups)
4 eggs, at room temperature,
separated
2 egg yolks
1 cup & 2 tablespoons
granulated sugar
2 tablespoons orange flower
water
$\frac{2}{3}$ cup candied peel, cut into
tiny pieces
unsalted butter for the pan
confectioners' sugar, for
decoration

At Easter time, bakers and pastry chefs in Naples compete with each other to produce the best *pastiere*, the beloved tart of the Neapolitans, made with whole wheat and ricotta. You can now buy whole wheat in cans, called Gran Pastiera, in good Italian grocers. It is good, and saves the long labor of soaking the grain.

1 If you are using dried whole wheat, soak the grains in cold water for 48 hours. Rinse and drain them.

2 Put the soaked wheat in a saucepan with the milk, salt, lemon and orange zest, the vanilla bean, and cinnamon and bring to a boil. Simmer over the lowest possible heat until the grain is cooked and tender, 3–4 hours. Let it cool at least 8 hours (24 hours is better) so the grain can swell. Remove and discard the vanilla bean.

3 If you are using canned wheat, just add the lemon and orange zest, vanilla extract, and cinnamon.

4 Make the pastry dough: sift the flour, sugar, and salt onto a work surface. Mix in the lemon zest, then rub in the butter. Add the egg yolks and knead together briefly to make a smooth and compact dough. (The dough can also be made in a food processor.) Wrap and chill at least 2 hours.

5 To make the filling, beat the ricotta with the 6 egg yolks. Add the granulated sugar, orange flower water, candied peel, and grain mixture. Mix very thoroughly.

6 Beat the 4 egg whites until stiff but not dry. Fold into the grain and ricotta mixture lightly but thoroughly.

7 Heat the oven to 350°F. Butter a 10-inch spring form cake pan. Roll out about two-thirds of the pastry dough and press into the pan, making sure it is of the same thickness all over the bottom and up the sides. Spoon in the filling.

8 Roll out the remaining dough and cut into long strips. Place the strips over the filling to form a lattice top. Bake until the filling is set and the pastry is golden brown, 45–50 minutes. Let the tart cool and then unmold it. Dust with sifted confectioners' sugar before serving.

For the pastry
2 cups all-purpose flour, preferably Italian 00 (see page 7)
6 tablespoons confectioners' sugar
pinch of salt
grated zest of $\frac{1}{2}$ lemon
10 tablespoons unsalted butter, cut into small pieces
3 extra large egg yolks

LA CROSTATA DI BIETOLE

SWISS CHARD AND CRÈME
PATISSIÈRE TART

Serves 6

For the pastry

1⅔ cups all-purpose flour,
preferably Italian 00 (see page 7)
4½ tablespoons granulated sugar
⅛ teaspoon salt
6 tablespoons unsalted butter
2 egg yolks
2 tablespoons hot milk

For the filling

1 pound Swiss chard
3 tablespoons granulated sugar
5 whole cloves
2 tablespoons golden raisins
2 tablespoons pine nuts
1 ounce semisweet chocolate,
cut into small pieces

For the crème patissière

1¼ cups whole milk
pared strip of unwaxed
lemon zest
pared strip of unwaxed
orange zest
1 cinnamon stick
piece of vanilla bean
2 egg yolks
2 tablespoons all-purpose flour
¼ cup granulated sugar
confectioners' sugar, for
decoration

I had this extraordinary tart at the San Martino restaurant in London. I find it extraordinary because of the use of Swiss chard in a sweet dish, something I have never met before. Yet the owner of the San Martino assured me that in his native province of Lucca the tart is called "La Torta della Nonna" – grandmother's tart, a name that proves its popularity.

It is quite delicious, as well as being mysterious in its remote chocolatey taste.

---

1 To make the pastry, pile the flour on the work surface, mix in the sugar and salt, and rub in the butter. Add the egg yolks and hot milk and work quickly to form a ball. Wrap and chill at least 2 hours.

2 Roll out two-thirds of the dough into a circle ¼-inch thick. Line a 7-inch loose-based tart pan with the circle of dough, pressing firmly into the corners. Put back into the refrigerator while you prepare the filling.

3 To make the crème patissière, put the milk in a saucepan, add all the flavorings, and bring to a boil. Draw off the heat and let infuse about 1 hour.

4 Put the egg yolks and sugar into a heavy-bottomed saucepan and beat until the eggs are pale yellow and creamy. Add the flour gradually.

5 Strain the milk and return to its pan. Bring back to simmering point. Off the heat, add very gradually to the egg and flour mixture, beating constantly.

6 Put the saucepan over low heat and bring to a simmer, while stirring constantly. Simmer 5 minutes to cook the flour and then draw off the heat. Place the base of the pan in cold water to cool quickly.

7 Remove the Swiss chard stems from the leaves; reserve the stems for another dish. Bring $1\frac{1}{4}$ cups of water to a boil. Add the granulated sugar and cloves and stir to dissolve the sugar. Plunge in the Swiss chard leaves, stir well, and cook until tender. Drain, but do not squeeze the liquid out. Set aside.

8 Heat the oven to 400°F.

9 Spread a little of the crème pâtissière over the bottom of the pastry. Cover with about half the Swiss chard and sprinkle with half the raisins, pine nuts, and chocolate pieces. Spread on another layer of crème, then more Swiss chard and finally the remaining crème. Sprinkle the remaining raisins, pine nuts, and chocolate pieces over the top.

10 Roll out the remaining pastry. Cut 6 strips, each about $\frac{1}{2}$-inch wide, and lay them o top of the tart in a criss-cross fashion to form a lattice. Bake until the pastry is golden brown, about 20 minutes. Let the tart cool in the pan. When cold, unmold and sprinkle the top with sifted confectioners' sugar.

BISCOTTI E FRITTELLE

COOKIES AND FRITTERS

If you open a regional Italian cook book, you will find more recipes for cookies than for any other type of sweetmeat. This is because, in Italy, desserts tend to be eaten at any time of day, whereas to have a dessert at the end of a meal is unusual. Cookies are often eaten casually, as a snack, with a glass of wine, sitting around the kitchen table.

From the vast range of sweet fritters in Italy, I have picked two recipes that I particularly like. Fritters are among the most ancient of foods; in Roman times they were prepared and eaten in the streets on pagan feast days, just as they are today at village feasts. Frying, after all, is the most immediate of cooking methods, and requires only a saucepan full of oil.

In all the cake and cookie recipes, I recommend the use of Italian 00 flour. This is a high-quality flour with very little flavor and very good raising properties. It is available from specialist Italian stores.

BACI DI DAMA
LADY'S KISSES

Makes about 35 cookies

1 cup almonds
$\frac{1}{2}$ cup & 2 tablespoons sugar
1 stick unsalted butter, at room temperature
1 teaspoon pure vanilla extract
pinch of salt
$\frac{3}{4}$ cup all-purpose flour, preferably Italian 00 (see page 27)
unsalted butter for the sheets
4 ounces semisweet chocolate

The name of these cookies is just as lovely as the cookies themselves. They are a specialty of Tortona, a town in southern Piedmont.

1 Heat the oven to 350°F.
2 Blanch the almonds in boiling water for 30 seconds. Drain and squeeze them in your fingers to remove the skins. Spread them on a baking sheet and dry thoroughly in the oven, about 5 minutes.
3 Put the almonds in a food processor. Add 2 tablespoons of the sugar (this absorbs the oil from the nuts) and process to a fine powder. Add the butter, vanilla, and salt and process again until the mixture is very creamy. Transfer to a bowl.
4 Sift the flour into the bowl. Fold in the flour very thoroughly to make a dough.
5 Break off pieces of the dough, the size of cherries, and roll them into balls between the palms of your hands. Place them on buttered baking sheets, spacing them about $\frac{3}{4}$ inch apart. Bake until golden brown, about 15 minutes. Let them cool on the sheets about 5 minutes and then transfer to a wire rack to cool completely.
6 Melt the chocolate in a bain-marie. When the cookies are cold, spread a little of the chocolate over half the cookies and make sandwiches by sticking another cookie to the chocolate.

I BISCOTTI DELLA NONNA CATERINA
MY GRANDMOTHER'S COOKIES

There is an infinite number of "Torte della Nonna," but unfortunately I can't claim any as <u>my</u> grandmother's. However, she made these lovely cookies that are ideal for serving with ice-creams or mousses, or to have with coffee.

1 Heat the oven to 350°F.

2 Beat the egg yolks with the rum. Add the sugar and beat hard until pale.

3 Sift the flour with the salt and add gradually to the egg and sugar mixture, stirring hard the whole time.

4 Add the butter and beat until the mixture is well blended.

5 Butter two baking sheets. To form the cookies dampen your hands, pick up a little dollop of the cookie dough, and shape it into a round. Place the rounds on the sheets, leaving about 2 inches between each one, because the dough spreads out a lot while cooking. Bake 15–20 minutes until deep gold.

6 Remove the sheets from the oven and transfer the cookies to a wire rack to cool.

These cookies will keep well a week in an airtight tin.

Makes about 24 cookies

2 extra large egg yolks
2 tablespoons rum
$\frac{1}{2}$ cup & 2 tablespoons sugar
1 cup all-purpose flour, preferably Italian 00 (see page 27)
pinch of salt
7 tablespoons unsalted butter, very soft but not melted
unsalted butter and flour for the sheets

LE BISSE

S-SHAPED COOKIES

Makes about 40 cookies

3 eggs
nearly 1 cup sugar
⅔ cup vegetable or olive oil
grated zest of 1 unwaxed lemon
3⅓ cups all-purpose flour,
preferably Italian 00 (see
page 27)
pinch of salt
oil for baking sheets

A *bissa* is a water snake in Venetian dialect, which explains the name of these little cookies. They are to be found in any bakery or *pasticceria* in Venice, but they can easily be made at home. Use an oil without flavor.

1 In a large bowl, beat the eggs with the sugar until pale and frothy. Add the oil and lemon zest, then fold in the flour and salt. Knead well. Wrap the dough and chill it about 1 hour.
2 Preheat the oven to 425°F.
3 Grease 2 large baking sheets with a little oil.
4 To shape each cookie take a little ball of dough and roll it into a sausage shape a little more than ½-inch thick and 5-inches long. Curve into the form of an "S" and set on a baking sheet.
5 Bake 5 minutes, then reduce the heat to 350°F and continue baking until pale golden, 10–15 minutes longer. Cool slightly on the baking sheets before transferring to a wire rack to cool completely.

CROSTOLI TRENTINI
FRITTERS FROM NORTHERN ITALY

At Carnival time, every bakery or *pasticceria* in northern and central Italy makes a show of huge trays piled high with puffy golden fritters sprinkled with confectioners' sugar. They are the traditional Carnival fare, made in different shapes in the various regions. Thus there are *cenci*, meaning rags, in Tuscany, *chiacchiere*, chatterings, in *Lombardy, galani*, ribbons, in Venice, and *sfrappole* in Emilia. The dough varies only a little. What changes is the shape.

The original crostoli from Trentino and Friuli are strips of dough tied in a loose knot, but they are often cut, as in my recipe, which is easier and quicker. If you serve them at the end of a meal, pass around a bowl of whipped cream to dollop over the crostoli.

Serves 6

1 cup all-purpose flour, preferably Italian 00 (see page 27)
1½ tablespoons granulated sugar
½ teaspoon baking powder
pinch of salt
2 tablespoons unsalted butter, at room temperature
1 extra large egg yolk
3 tablespoons grappa (Italian eau-de-vie) or white rum
1–2 tablespoons low-fat milk
oil for frying
confectioners' sugar, for decoration

1 Set aside 2 tablespoons of flour. Put the rest of the flour on a work surface. Mix in the granulated sugar, baking powder, and salt. Make a well and put in the butter, egg yolk, grappa, and milk. Mix everything together, kneading until the dough is well blended. If it is too hard add a little more milk; if too soft add some of the reserved flour. You can also make the dough in a food processor.

2 Knead the dough at least 5 minutes as you would with bread or pasta dough. The dough should become smooth and elastic. Make a ball, wrap, and leave at room temperature for 1 hour or longer.

3 Roll out the dough <u>very</u> thinly, using either a rolling pin or, better, a hand-cranked pasta machine. If you are using the machine, roll through the last setting. The thinness of the dough is the secret of good crostoli.

4 Using a pastry wheel, cut the strips of dough into lasagne-size rectangles. Make 3 parallel slashes in the middle of each rectangle.

5 Heat enough frying oil to come two-thirds of the way up the sides of a frying pan or a wok. When the oil is very hot (a piece of stale bread should take 50 seconds to brown), fry the dough shapes in batches until pale gold and puffy. Lift the crostoli out of the oil with a slotted spatula and place on paper towels to drain.

6 Before serving, pile the crostoli on a dish, sprinkling every layer lavishly with sifted confectioners' sugar. They are excellent hot or cold.

FRITTELLE DI SEMOLINO

SEMOLINA FRITTERS

These are other Carnival fritters from northern Italy. In my home they were always served with apple fritters and, of course, crostoli (see previous recipe).

1 Bring the milk slowly to the simmer with the granulated sugar, lemon zest, butter, and salt, stirring frequently to dissolve the sugar.

2 Add the semolina in a slow stream while beating hard with a wooden spoon to prevent lumps forming. Continue stirring and cooking over low heat for 10 minutes. The mixture will be quite stiff. Draw off the heat and let cool 15 minutes or so. Remove and discard the lemon zest.

3 Mix in the egg yolks, one at a time, beating well to incorporate after each addition.

4 Spread the semolina mixture on a board or flat dish to a thickness of about 1 inch. Level it down evenly with a damp spatula and let it cool completely. You can leave it overnight.

5 Cut the semolina into 1-inch-wide strips and then cut the strips across to make lozenges.

6 Heat oil in a wok or in a deep frying pan to 330°F – hot enough for a cube of stale bread to brown in 50 seconds.

7 Meanwhile, lightly beat the 2 whole eggs in a bowl and spread the bread crumbs in a dish. Dip a piece of semolina into the egg and then coat with bread crumbs, patting them into the semolina.

8 Fry, in 2 or 3 batches, to a lovely gold color and then put into a dish lined with paper towels to drain.

9 Serve hot or cold, lavishly sprinkled with sifted confectioners' sugar.

Makes about 24 fritters

1 quart whole milk
$\frac{1}{2}$ cup granulated sugar
pared strip of unwaxed lemon zest
1 stick unsalted butter
pinch of salt
$1\frac{1}{2}$ cups semolina flour
3 extra large egg yolks
oil for frying
2 eggs
2 cups dry bread crumbs
confectioners' sugar, for decoration

DOLCI AL CUCCHIAIO

FRUIT AND CREAM DESSERTS

In this section I have collected eight recipes for dolci that are served at dinner parties, some famous, some little known, some elaborate and rich, others simple and modest, but all good and typically Italian.

TIRAMISU

———— MASCARPONE AND COFFEE DESSERT ————

Serves 6

$\frac{2}{3}$ cup strong espresso coffee
3 tablespoons brandy
2 ounces semisweet chocolate
2 eggs, at room temperature,
separated
1 egg yolk
$\frac{1}{4}$ cup sugar
9 ounces mascarpone cheese
(1 heaped cup)
about 20 Savoiardi cookies

For the decoration
coffee beans
candied violets (optional)

A book on dolci would hardly be complete without including the most popular of them all, Tiramisù (whose literal meaning is "pick-me-up"). Surprisingly, considering its popularity, Tiramisù is a relatively new arrival even on the Italian scene. Up to 20 years ago it was only known in the region where it originated, the Veneto.

Savoiardi are available from Italian grocers. If you cannot find them, make your own ladyfinger cookies – ordinary ladyfingers from a supermarket will not be absorbent enough.

1 Mix together the coffee and brandy
2 Grate about one-quarter of the chocolate and cut the rest into small pieces.
3 Beat the 3 egg yolks with the sugar until very pale and softly peaked. Fold the mascarpone in gradually and mix very thoroughly until the mixture is smooth and does not show any lumps.
4 Beat the 2 egg whites until stiff but not dry and fold gradually into the mascarpone and egg yolk mixture.
5 Dip the cookies, one at a time, into the coffee and brandy mixture, turning them over once or twice until they become pale brown. Lay 7 cookies on the bottom of an oval dish, so as to make a base. Spread over one-quarter of the mascarpone cream and scatter with some chocolate pieces. Dip more cookies into the coffee mixture and make another layer. Spread with another quarter of the cream and scatter with chocolate pieces. Cover with the last layer of moistened cookies and spread with half the remaining cream.

6 Cover the dish tightly and put it, with the reserved mascarpone cream, in the refrigerator to chill about 6 hours.

7 Before serving, spread the reserved mascarpone cream over the top, smoothing it down neatly with a spatula. Sprinkle the grated chocolate all over the top and decorate with the coffee beans and with the optional candied violets.

CREMA MASCARPONE
MASCARPONE AND RUM CREAM

Similar to the ubiquitous Tiramisù, this dessert is lighter and more subtle. In my family it used to be called "La Crema del Principe", and it is indeed a royal dessert, smooth and delicate.

The cream can be prepared ahead of time up to step 3. Add the egg whites no longer than 1 hour before serving. Serve with amaretti cookies, whose dark, almondy flavor is ideal with this dessert.

Serves 4

2 eggs, separated
2 tablespoons sugar
2 tablespoons dark rum
$\frac{1}{2}$ pound mascarpone cheese
(1 cup)
1 teaspoon lemon juice
12 amaretti cookies

1 Beat the egg yolks with the sugar until light and mousse-like, then beat in the rum.

2 Press the mascarpone through a fine strainer and fold into the egg yolk mixture.

3 Beat the egg whites with the lemon juice until stiff but not dry and fold gently into the mixture until the cream is smooth. Spoon the mixture into long stem glasses and place 1 amaretto on the top. Pass the rest of the amaretti around on a plate. Keep the cream chilled until ready to serve.

LA MERINGA FARCITA
MERINGUE FILLED WITH MARRONS GLACÉS,
CHOCOLATE, AND CREAM

Serves 6–8

For the meringue

4 extra large egg whites, at room
temperature
1 teaspoon lemon juice
1 cup & 2 tablespoons sugar

For the filling

2 extra large egg whites
3 tablespoons sugar
2 cups whipping cream
$\frac{1}{4}$ cup dark rum
$\frac{1}{2}$ pound marrons glacés (candied
chestnuts), cut into small pieces
4 ounces semisweet chocolate,
cut into small pieces
2 tablespoons pistachio nuts,
blanched, peeled and chopped
(see page 52)

The meringue in this recipe is Italian meringue, which is more reliable and less fragile than Swiss meringue made with uncooked whites of egg.

---

1 Heat the oven to 300°F.

2 Make an Italian meringue as follows. Beat the egg whites with the lemon juice until stiff. Put the bowl over a saucepan of simmering water and continue beating while gradually adding the sugar. Beat until the mixture is warm, silky looking, and forming soft peaks.

3 Draw two 8-inch circles on parchment paper. Place the paper on 1 or 2 baking sheets. Spoon the meringue over the two circles, smoothing it out with a metal spatula. Place the sheets in the oven and bake until the meringue is set, about 45 minutes. Remove the meringue disks from the paper and let them cool.

4 For the filling, beat the egg whites in a bowl until stiff. Place the bowl over a saucepan of simmering water and gradually add the sugar, while beating constantly. When the mixture is warm, remove from the heat and place the base of the bowl in cold water to cool. This stiff egg white mixture makes the filling lighter, both in texture and in substance.

5 Whip the cream. Fold in the egg white mixture.

6 Add the rum, marrons glacés, chocolate, and pistachios and mix well until everything is evenly distributed.

7 Place one of the meringue disks on a serving plate. Spread two-thirds of the filling over it and put the other disk on top. Cover with the remaining filling. Chill at least 6 hours before serving.

LE DITA DEGLI APOSTOLI
CRÊPES STUFFED WITH RICOTTA

The odd name of this recipe from Puglia, the heel of the Italian boot, means Apostles' Fingers. I can only suppose the crêpes were given this name because their appearance calls to mind long fingers, raised to give a blessing.

This is the recipe developed by my colleague and dear friend, Alice Wooledge Salmon, from the original recipe by the cookery teacher, Paola Pettini, who showed us how to make the Dita during a recent stay in Puglia.

1 To make the crêpes, beat the eggs with the sugar. Mix in the flour and salt and then gradually add the milk while beating constantly. The batter should be fairly liquid. Let it rest 1 hour.

2 Meanwhile prepare the stuffing. Press the ricotta through a strainer into a bowl and fold in the cream and granulated sugar. Add all the other ingredients and mix very thoroughly. Chill.

3 Make very thin crêpes in an 11-inch pan (if not using a nonstick pan, grease it lightly with melted butter). You should get 12 large crêpes.

4 Lay the crêpes on the work surface and spread the stuffing thinly all over each one. Roll them tightly.

5 Cut each "finger" into 3 or 4 pieces, place on a dish, and sprinkle with sifted confectioners' sugar. They are traditionally served cold.

Serves 8–10

For the crêpes
5 eggs
2½ tablespoons granulated sugar
¾ cup all-purpose flour
pinch of salt
1 cup low-fat milk
butter for frying crêpes

For the stuffing
1¼ pounds fresh ricotta cheese
(2½ cups)
3 tablespoons whipping cream
1¼ cups granulated sugar
grated zest of 1 unwaxed lemon
grated zest of 1 unwaxed orange
grated zest of 1 unwaxed
clementine
1½ tablespoons finely chopped
candied peel
2 ounces semisweet chocolate,
cut into small pieces
2 tablespoons dark rum
confectioners' sugar, for
decoration

MELE ALLE MANDORLE E AL VINO BIANCO

SAUTÉED APPLES WITH ALMONDS AND WHITE WINE

Serves 6

6 equal-sized large apples such as Granny Smith
1 unwaxed lemon, scrubbed and washed
4 tablespoons unsalted butter
3 cloves
$\frac{2}{3}$ cup Calvados or applejack
$\frac{1}{4}$ cup granulated sugar, or more according to the sweetness of the apples
$\frac{1}{2}$ cup sweet white wine
$\frac{1}{2}$ teaspoon ground cinnamon
1 cup sliced almonds
$1\frac{1}{4}$ cups whipping cream
$\frac{1}{4}$ cup confectioners' sugar, sifted

A lovely dessert, this combines the light, fresh flavor of fruit with the richness of a brandy-laced cream.

1 Peel the apples, then cut them in half and remove the cores. Make 6 incisions in the round side of each half, taking care not to cut right through it.

2 Remove the zest from half the lemon using a swivel-headed vegetable peeler, taking care to leave behind the bitter white pith. Squeeze the juice.

3 Heat the butter in a very large sauté pan in which the apple halves will fit comfortably. Add the lemon zest and cloves to the butter and when the butter foam begins to subside, slide in the apples, cut-side down. Sauté until golden, then turn the halves over and brown the round side. This will take about 8 minutes. Shake the pan occasionally to prevent the apples sticking.

4 Turn the heat up, pour over one-third of the Calvados, and let it bubble away for 30 seconds. Turn the heat down to low and add the granulated sugar, wine, lemon juice, and $\frac{2}{3}$ cup of hot water. Cover the pan with the lid or a piece of foil and cook 5 minutes. Turn the apples over carefully and continue cooking until they are tender. Cooking time varies according to the quality of the apples; do not overcook them or they may break. If necessary add a couple of spoonsful of hot water during the cooking.

5 When the apples are ready – test them by piercing them with the blade of a small knife through their thickest part – transfer them gently to a dish using a slotted spoon. Let cool.

6 Remove the lemon zest and cloves from the pan. Add the cinnamon and almonds and sauté over medium heat, stirring constantly, until the syrup is thick and the almonds are caramelized, about 5 minutes. Draw off the heat.

7 Whip the cream. Add the remaining Calvados and the confectioners' sugar and whip again. Spread the cream over a shallow serving dish. Make 12 hollows in the cream with the back of a spoon and lay the apple halves in the hollows, cut-side up. Spoon the syrup-coated almonds over the apples. Serve at room temperature.

FRUTTA COTTA AL FORNO
COMPÔTE OF MIXED FRUIT

The simplicity of this dessert should not deter you from trying it. The fruit, well cooked yet still in neat pieces, absorbs the flavor of the wine that, through the long cooking, has lost the taste of alcohol, which can be unpleasant when cooked with food. Buy prunes that don't need to be soaked.

Serves 4

1 pear, preferably Comice or Bartlett
2 apples, such as Granny Smith
1 banana
2 oranges
6 pitted prunes
grated zest of 1 small lemon
3 tablespoons sugar
$\frac{1}{2}$ cup robust red wine, such as Barbera

1 Heat the oven to 350°F.

2 Peel and core the pear and apples. Peel the banana and oranges. Slice them all quite thinly, keeping them separate.

3 Lay the sliced fruit in layers in a 1-quart baking dish, arranging it so that each fruit is topped with a different fruit. Scatter the prunes here and there and sprinkle with the lemon zest and sugar. Pour the wine over the top and cover the dish. Bake 30 minutes.

4 Uncover the dish and press the fruit down with a slotted spoon to release more liquid. Bake 15 minutes longer. Serve warm, with or without cream.

ZUCCOTTO

FLORENTINE CREAM PUDDING

Serves 8–10

$\frac{1}{2}$ cup almonds, blanched and
peeled (see page 28)
$\frac{1}{2}$ cup hazelnuts
3 tablespoons brandy
3 tablespoons Amaretto liqueur
3 tablespoons Maraschino or
other sweet liqueur
9 ounces pound cake, cut into
$\frac{1}{4}$-inch-thick slices
5 ounces semisweet chocolate
2 cups whipping cream
$\frac{3}{4}$ cup confectioners' sugar, sifted

For the decoration
2 tablespoons confectioners'
sugar
1 tablespoon unsweetened
cocoa powder, sifted

A rich, creamy pudding from Florence. Its domed shape is like half a pumpkin (*zucca* in Italian) and it is decorated with alternate brown and white segments, like the cupola of Florence cathedral.

1 Heat the oven to 400°F. Put the almonds and hazelnuts on separate baking sheets and toast in the oven 5 minutes. Then, with a rough towel, rub off as much of the hazelnut skins as you can. Roughly chop the almonds and hazelnuts and set aside.
2 Mix the three liqueurs together. Line the inside of a $1\frac{1}{2}$-quart pudding basin or domed mold with plastic wrap and then with cake slices reserving some for the top. Moisten the cake with most of the liqueur mixture.
3 Melt 2 ounces of the chocolate in a small bowl set over a pan of simmering water; set aside. Cut the remaining chocolate into small pieces.
4 Whip the cream with the confectioners' sugar until stiff. Fold in the almonds, hazelnuts, and chocolate pieces.
5 Divide the cream mixture in half and spoon one portion into the mold, spreading it evenly all over the cake lining the bottom and sides. Fold the melted chocolate into the remaining cream mixture and spoon it into the mold to fill the cavity. Cover the pudding with the reserved cake and moisten it with the rest of the liqueur. Cover the mold with plastic wrap and refrigerate at least 12 hours.
6 To unmold place a piece of wax paper and then a piece of cardboard over the top of the pudding basin. Turn the basin over to unmold the pudding onto the paper and cardboard. Place on a board, remove the basin, and peel off the plastic wrap.

7 To decorate the pudding, cut out a circle of wax paper 15 inches in diameter. Fold in two to make a half moon, then fold this in two to make a triangle. Fold the triangle in two again to make a thinner triangle. Open out and cut out each alternate section, without cutting through the paper at the top.

8 Dust the whole dome with some sifted confectioners' sugar. Mix 2 tablespoons of sifted confectioners' sugar with the cocoa. Place the cut-out circle of paper over the dome and sprinkle the cocoa and sugar mixture in the cut-out sections. Remove the paper carefully without spoiling the pattern. Transfer the pudding to a round serving plate, using the cardboard for support. Serve chilled.

ZUPPA INGLESE
CAKE AND CUSTARD PUDDING

Serves 6

⅔ cup whipping cream
¾ pound cake, cut in ¼-inch slices
¼ cup rum
¼ cup cherry brandy
2 egg whites, at room
temperature
⅓ cup confectioners' sugar, sifted
1 tablespoon granulated sugar

For the custard

2 cups whole milk
2 strips of lemon zest
3 egg yolks
6 tablespoons granulated sugar
⅓ cup all-purpose flour

Zuppa Inglese used to be on almost every menu in restaurants within Italy and elsewhere, just as Tiramisù is today. And, like Tiramisù, it can be delicious or a disaster. It all depends on the light balance of the ingredients used.

The name Zuppa Inglese – English soup – is a mystery. Like other Italian writers on the subject, I think the pudding must owe its origin to English trifle, which would have been brought to Tuscany and Naples by the English in the eighteenth and nineteenth centuries.

The liqueur Alchermes, used in Italy, is hardly available elsewhere. Cherry brandy is a good substitute.

---

1 First make the custard. Bring the milk to a boil, with the lemon zest and set aside.

2 Beat the egg yolks with the sugar until pale yellow and light. Beat the flour into the mixture and then slowly pour in the hot milk.

3 Transfer the custard to a heavy-bottomed saucepan and place over very low heat. Cook, stirring the whole time, until the custard becomes very thick and an occasional bubble breaks through the surface. Simmer very gently a couple of minutes longer. Place the base of the saucepan in ice water to cool the custard quickly. Stir frequently.

4 Whip the cream until soft peaks form. When the custard is cold, fold in the cream.

5 Choose a soufflé dish of 7 cup capacity and line it with plastic wrap, wax paper, or parchment paper, which will help in unmolding the pudding.

6 Line the bottom of the soufflé dish with slices of cake, plugging any holes with pieces of cake. Sprinkle with some rum and spread a couple of spoonsfuls of custard over the cake.

7 Cover with another layer of cake, moisten it with cherry brandy, and then spread over some custard. Repeat these layers, ending with the cake moistened with one of the liqueurs.

8 Cover the pudding with plastic wrap, place it in the refrigerator, and chill at least 8 hours, or better still 24 hours, to let all the flavors combine.

9 Some 6 hours before you want to serve the pudding, heat the oven to 225°F. Beat the egg whites with the confectioners' sugar until stiff. Remove the pudding from the refrigerator and unmold it onto a round serving plate that can be put in the oven at a low temperature. Spread the meringue all over the pudding and sprinkle with the granulated sugar. Bake until the meringue is dry and very pale blond in color about $\frac{1}{4}$ hour to 20 minutes. Let cool and then replace the pudding in the refrigerator to chill at least 2 hours before serving.

GELATI, SORBETTI E GELATINE

ICE CREAMS, SORBETS, AND FRUIT GELATINS

I could write a whole book on these desserts, so choosing just a few recipes was quite difficult. Gelati and sorbetti had their origins in Italy, and it was the Italian emigrants who took them to the USA, where people have now adopted them and made them their own.

I find that only in Italy can you still find excellent ices in specialist *gelaterie* – ice cream shops where the ice creams are made on the premises. The choice is bewildering. Some new favorite flavors, such as tiramisù and zuppa inglese, compete with the lovely old classics, gelato al caffè or al limone. The fruit water-ices are the best because of the strong flavor of the fruit, ripened in the hot sun.

Fruit gelatins are now making a welcome come-back on the tables of health-conscious people, and I have included two recipes for them at the end of this section.

SPUMONE AL CIOCCOLATO

FROZEN CHOCOLATE CREAM LOAF

Serves 8

5 ounces semisweet chocolate
$1\frac{1}{2}$ cups whole milk
4 egg yolks
$\frac{1}{2}$ cup & 2 tablespoons sugar
4 teaspoons all-purpose flour
$\frac{1}{4}$ cup strong espresso coffee
$1\frac{1}{4}$ cups whipping cream, very cold
12 amaretti cookies (optional)
$\frac{1}{2}$ cup Marsala or medium sherry wine (optional)

A *spumone* is a kind of soft ice cream. Spumoni are always molded in a pan, usually a loaf pan, and served cut into slices like a pâté. This is the recipe for a chocolate spumone of a delicate creamy flavor. You need the best quality chocolate with a high cocoa butter content.

This spumone is particularly delicious covered with amaretti that have been lightly soaked in Marsala or sherry.

---

1 Melt the chocolate in a bain-marie.

2 Heat the milk to simmering point.

3 Meanwhile, beat the egg yolks with the sugar until pale and light. Add the flour and beat well. Slowly pour in the hot milk, while beating constantly. Transfer the custard to a heavy-bottomed saucepan and cook over the lowest heat, stirring constantly, until the custard thickens and some bubbles break on the surface. Cook a couple of minutes longer, never ceasing to stir.

4 Mix the melted chocolate and the coffee into the custard. Put the base of the saucepan in cold water to cool the custard quickly. Stir every now and then.

5 Whip the cream. When the custard is cold, fold in the cream.

6 Line a $1\frac{1}{2}$-quart loaf pan with plastic wrap, foil, or wax paper. Spoon the mixture into the pan and freeze overnight.

7 Remove from the freezer 1 hour before serving. Unmold onto a rectangular plate and cut in slices to serve.

Note: If you wish to cover the ice cream with amaretti, dip the cookies briefly in the Marsala or sherry and lay them over the spumone just before serving.

SEMIFREDDO DI ZABAGLIONE AL CAFFE
FROZEN COFFEE ZABAGLIONE

A "semifreddo" cannot be frozen hard because of the high sugar content in the meringue. This why it is called "half-cold," and why its consistency is so soft and voluptuous.

1 In the upper part of a double boiler or in a heatproof bowl, beat the 5 egg yolks with the granulated sugar until pale and thick. Add the cinnamon and Marsala or sherry and continue beating for a minute or so.

2 Put some water in the lower part of the double boiler or in a saucepan in which the bowl can be placed. Turn the heat on and put in place the top of the double boiler or the bowl containing the egg yolk mixture. Beat the mixture constantly while it heats, until it becomes a soft, foamy mess. Remove from the heat and add the coffee. Place in a sink of cold water to cool. Stir the zabaglione every now and then to prevent a skin forming.

3 Whip the cream and fold into the zabaglione lightly but thoroughly.

4 Beat the egg whites until firm. Gradually add the confectioners' sugar and continue beating until the meringue forms stiff peaks. Fold it, 1 or 2 spoonfuls at a time, into the egg-yolk mixture.

5 Spoon the zabaglione into a glass bowl or individual glasses and freeze overnight.

6 Decorate with candied coffee beans and whipped cream before serving.

Serves 6

3 eggs, separated
2 egg yolks
$\frac{1}{2}$ cup + 2 tablespoons granulated sugar
pinch of ground cinnamon
$\frac{2}{3}$ cup Marsala or medium sweet sherry wine
$\frac{1}{4}$ cup strong espresso coffee
1 cup whipping cream
$\frac{3}{4}$ cup confectioners' sugar, sifted
candied coffee beans and whipped cream, for decoration

SORBETTO AL MANDARINO
MANDARIN SORBET

Serves 4

nearly 1 cup sugar
pared zest of 1 unwaxed lemon,
without any white pith
pared zest of 1 unwaxed orange,
without any white pith
$1\frac{1}{4}$ cups freshly squeezed
mandarin juice
$\frac{1}{4}$ cup freshly squeezed
orange juice
$\frac{1}{4}$ cup freshly squeezed
lemon juice
2 tablespoons white rum

Mandarins are a type of orange that have easy-to-peel skin. The tangerine is the most common mandarin orange in the US, although you can also sometimes find clementines, with their sweet-tart flesh, and seedless satsumas. Any of these can be used to make this sorbet. It can also be made with fresh orange juice to which the juice of a lemon is added.

1 Put the sugar, lemon and orange zest, and $1\frac{1}{4}$ cups of water in a heavy-bottomed saucepan. Bring slowly to a boil and simmer 5 minutes. Let cool, then strain the syrup.
2 Strain the fruit juices and add to the cold syrup with the rum. Mix well and pour the mixture into an ice cream machine. Freeze according to the manufacturer's instructions.

CASSATA GELATA
ICED CASSATA

Serves 6–8

$2\frac{1}{2}$ cups whole milk
grated zest of 1 unwaxed lemon
5 egg yolks
$\frac{3}{4}$ cup granulated sugar
3 tablespoons almonds
3 tablespoons pistachio nuts
$\frac{2}{3}$ cup whipping cream
3 tablespoons chopped candied
fruit or candied peel
1 tablespoon confectioners'
sugar, sifted

This is the original, homemade, recipe for the cassata that is now sold frozen in supermarkets. It is quite a lengthy dish to make, but it is easy, even if you do not have an ice-cream machine.

You can substitute bits of chocolate for the pistachio nuts.

1 Heat the milk to simmering point with the lemon zest.
2 Put the egg yolks and granulated sugar in a bowl (metal, if possible, as this will transmit heat and cold more quickly) and beat until pale and mousse-like. I use a hand-held electric mixer.

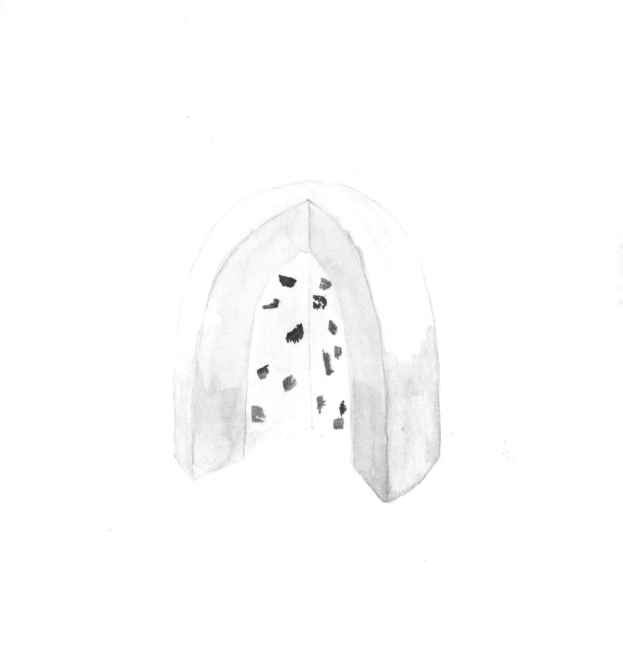

Then place the bowl over a saucepan of gently simmering water. Add the hot milk while beating the whole time. Cook until the custard thickens and will coat the back of a spoon. This can easily take as long as 25 minutes. Stir constantly and do not allow the custard to boil or the egg will curdle.

3 As soon as the custard is ready, draw from the heat and set the base of the bowl in cold water. Let cool, stirring frequently. When the custard is cold, strain it to remove the lemon zest, then freeze in an ice cream machine following the manufacturer's instructions. Or, still-freeze in the freezer. Do not freeze hard.

4 Place 5-cup bombe mold (or a metal mold and a piece of foil to act as a lid) in the freezer to chill 30 minutes.

5 Spoon the custard ice cream into the chilled mold, lining the bottom and sides evenly but leaving a hole in the middle. Return the mold to the freezer.

6 Blanch the almonds in boiling water 30 seconds and then squeeze them in your fingers to remove the skins. Dry and chop them coarsely. Do the same with the pistachio nuts.

7 Whip the cream and fold in the almonds, pistachios, candied fruit, and confectioners' sugar. Spoon this mixture into the center of the ice cream mold and return it to the freezer. Freeze at least 4 hours.

8 About 1 hour before serving, remove the lid from the mold, cover the mold with a serving plate, and turn them over. Put the mold, on the plate, in the refrigerator. By the time you want to serve the cassata you should be able to lift the mold off easily. If the cassata is still frozen onto the mold, dip the mold quickly into very hot water for a few seconds.

GELATINE DI FRUTTA

The image of fruit gelatins has been debased by the synthetic-tasting gelatins made from packages of flavored powder dissolved in water. In Italy these do not exist; the Italians have always made their fruit gelatins from the juice of the fresh fruit. These were particularly popular in the Renaissance, when they were made in various shapes and guises to become the centerpieces of lavishly adorned tables.

Here are two fruit gelatins, one for the summer and one for the winter. I use leaf gelatin, not gelatin powder, because it does not have the unpleasant gluey flavor of the powder, and because it dissolves more evenly. Leaf gelatin is sold in the best supermarkets and speciality food stores.

GELATINA DI ARANCIA

ORANGE GELATIN

Serves 4–6

¾ ounce leaf gelatin
¾ cup sugar
1¼ cups freshly squeezed orange juice, strained
¼ cup freshly squeezed lemon juice, strained
2 tablespoons Grand Marnier
¼ cup white rum

Buy oranges with full flavor and the right amount of acidity. I use only Italian or Spanish oranges, which have these attributes.

1 Soak the gelatin leaves in cold water at least 30 minutes.
2 Put the sugar and the strained fruit juices in a saucepan. Bring very slowly to a boil and simmer until the sugar has dissolved, stirring occasionally. Draw off the heat.
3 Put $\frac{7}{8}$ cup of water in a saucepan. Lift the gelatin leaves out of the soaking water and squeeze out the liquid. Add to the pan of water and heat gently until the gelatin has dissolved, beating constantly with a small wire balloon whisk. Pour into the fruit syrup and add the two liqueurs. Stir very thoroughly and let cool.

4 Grease a 3-cup decorative mold with a non-tasting vegetable oil or with almond oil. Pour the mixture into the mold and chill overnight or at least 6 hours.

5 To unmold, immerse the mold a few seconds in warm water. Place a serving plate over the mold and turn the whole thing upside down. Pat the mold and give a few jerks to the plate. The gelatin should now unmold easily. Put the mold back on the gelatin to cover it and replace the dish in the refrigerator until ready to serve.

I like to serve this orange gelatin with sliced oranges topped with passion fruit. For 4 people you will need 4–5 oranges, 2 tablespoons sugar, and 3 passion fruits. Peel the oranges to the quick and slice very thinly. Put them in a bowl and gently mix in the sugar. Cut the passion fruits in half and, with a pointed teaspoon, scoop out the little green seeds and the juice, spreading them all over the orange slices. Make the dish at least 2 hours in advance and keep it refrigerated, covered with plastic wrap.

GELATINA DI MORE O DI RIBES
—— BLACKBERRY OR RED CURRANT GELATIN ——

Serves 4–5

$\frac{3}{4}$ ounce leaf gelatin
$\frac{1}{2}$ cup & 2 tablespoons sugar
piece of vanilla bean, 2-inches
long
$1\frac{1}{4}$ cups pure blackberry or red
currant juice
$\frac{1}{4}$ cup Marsala wine
juice of $\frac{1}{2}$ lemon
$\frac{2}{3}$ cup whipping cream

This is a thick gelatin, rich in color and flavor, suitable for serving in individual bowls. I suggest you make your own fruit juice by boiling the fruit 2–3 minutes and then straining it through a strainer lined with cheesecloth.

1 Soak the gelatin leaves in cold water at least 30 minutes.

2 Put the sugar, $\frac{1}{2}$ cup of water, and the vanilla bean in a small saucepan. Bring slowly to a boil, stirring frequently. Simmer 10 minutes.

3 Squeeze the water out of the gelatin leaves. Add the gelatin to the sugar syrup and let it dissolve, while whisking constantly.

4 When the gelatin is thoroughly dissolved, draw the pan off the heat. Remove and discard the vanilla bean. Add the fruit juice, Marsala, and lemon juice and mix very thoroughly.

5 Spoon the fruit syrup into 4 or 5 bowls. Chill in the refrigerator at least 6 hours.

6 Whip the cream and drop a spoonful on top of each bowl. Return to refrigerator until you are ready to serve.

LIST OF RECIPES